DK SUPER Planet

Beautiful
BIODIVERSITY

Our planet supports an abundance of life—discover
the beauty and wonder of its biodiversity, from
forest floors to backyard ponds

Produced for DK by
Editorial Just Content Limited
Design Studio Noel

Author Lola M. Schaefer

Senior Editor Amelia Jones
Senior Art Editor Gilda Pacitti
Managing Editor Katherine Neep
Managing Art Editor Sarah Corcoran
Production Editor Jaypal Chauhan
DTP Designer Rohit Singh
Production Controller Rebecca Parton
Publisher Sarah Forbes
Managing Director, Learning Hilary Fine

First American Edition, 2025
Published in the United States by DK Publishing,
a division of Penguin Random House LLC
1745 Broadway, 20th Floor, New York, NY 10019

Copyright © 2025 Dorling Kindersley Limited
25 26 27 28 29 10 9 8 7 6 5 4 3 2 1
001–345528–Apr/2025

A catalog record for this book is
available from the Library of Congress.
HC ISBN: 978-0-5939-6610-5
PB ISBN: 978-0-5939-6609-9

DK books are available at special discounts when purchased
in bulk for sales promotions, premiums, fund-raising,
or educational use.
For details, contact: DK Publishing Special Markets,
1745 Broadway, 20th Floor, New York, NY 10019
SpecialSales@dk.com

Printed and bound in China

www.dk.com

This book was made with Forest
Stewardship Council™ certified
paper – one small step in DK's
commitment to a sustainable future.
**Learn more at www.dk.com/uk/
information/sustainability**

Contents

Words in **bold** are explained in the glossary on page 44.

What is BIODIVERSITY?

There are many **ecosystems** in the world, like dry deserts and green rainforests. These **habitats** are home to lots of living things. **Biodiversity** is the amount of different life forms in an ecosystem. It is also how living things connect with each other and their **environment**. An ecosystem with a lot of biodiversity is healthy and balanced.

Polar bears live in the Arctic. Even though it is very cold, the Arctic is full of biodiversity. It is home to thousands of living **species** that thrive in the icy conditions.

Peru is one of the most biodiverse countries in the world. It contains habitats like rainforests and mountains that make it a special place for plants and animals.

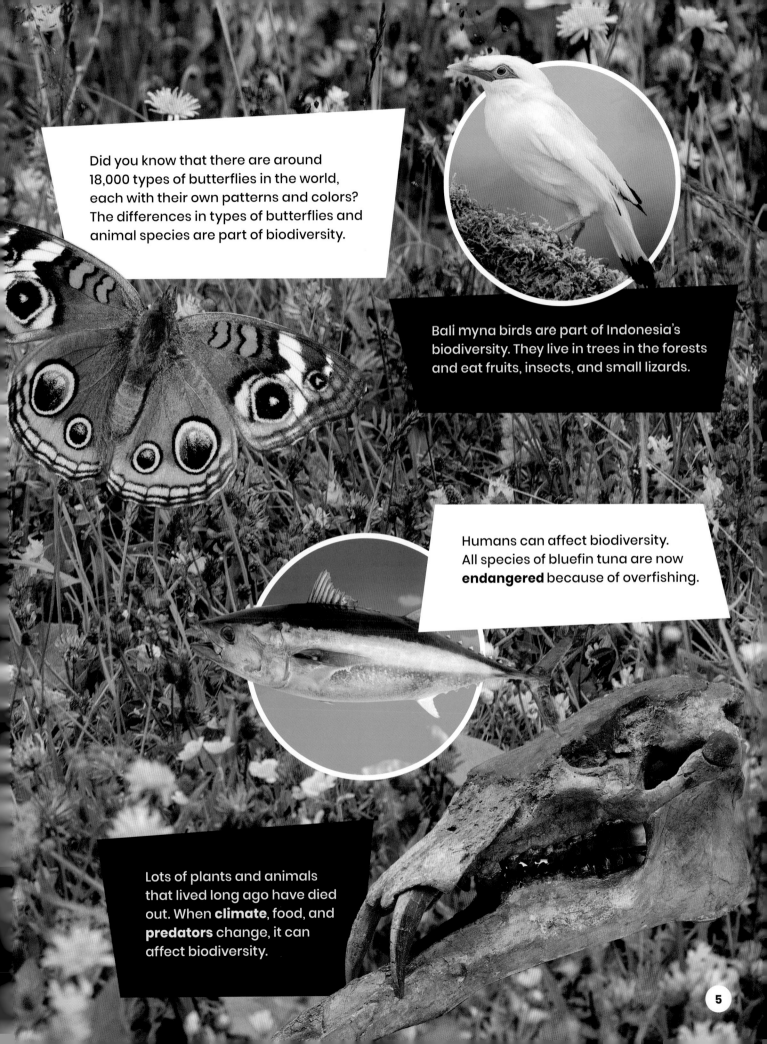

Did you know that there are around 18,000 types of butterflies in the world, each with their own patterns and colors? The differences in types of butterflies and animal species are part of biodiversity.

Bali myna birds are part of Indonesia's biodiversity. They live in trees in the forests and eat fruits, insects, and small lizards.

Humans can affect biodiversity. All species of bluefin tuna are now **endangered** because of overfishing.

Lots of plants and animals that lived long ago have died out. When **climate**, food, and **predators** change, it can affect biodiversity.

A Journey of
DISCOVERY

You can find biodiversity in many different ecosystems, such as rivers filled with fish and frogs, forests buzzing with birds and insects, and even rooftop gardens in cities. Let's go on an exciting adventure to discover biodiversity around the world. As we explore, we will see how people are working to protect and restore different habitats, helping all kinds of plants and animals thrive.

Scientists have found 1.2 million species of plants and animals on Earth. They think there might be 6 or 7 million more they have yet to discover.

Fascinating fact

The Sonoran Desert has the most biodiversity of any desert ecosystem on Earth. There are animals like javelinas, coyotes and bobcats, as well as over 300 species of birds and more than 100 species of reptiles.

Spider monkeys live in tropical rainforests. They spend most of their time high up in the trees. This helps them to find food and to avoid predators.

All life forms need biodiversity to survive. Healthy, balanced ecosystems give living things what they need, like food and shelter.

When it is scared, the Madagascar tenrec rolls into a ball. It points its spines in every direction. This protects it from predators and other dangers, and helps it survive.

Arctic snowshoe hares use **camouflage** to survive. In the winter, their fur is white like snow. In the summer, it turns brown.

Under the
MICROSCOPE

Some living things are so tiny you cannot see them with the eye. They can only be seen using a special tool called a **microscope**. Some of these tiny **organisms** include **algae**, **bacteria**, and **mold**. They are found in the soil, air, and water. They are an important part of the biodiversity of an ecosystem.

Scientists who study organisms such as bacteria are called microbiologists. They try to find out how to prevent and treat diseases.

Fascinating fact

Around 100 trillion bacteria live in your digestive system. There are bacteria that help you stay healthy, as well as bacteria that can make you sick.

Birds like the green wood hoopoe produce oil that is rich in good bacteria. This oil keeps their feathers clean and healthy by coating them during **preening**. The bacteria in the oil create a special barrier, protecting the feathers from other harmful bacteria that could cause damage.

All the plants and animals on Earth have tiny organisms that live on and inside them. This is called a **microbiome**. Each one is **unique**.

1,000,000,000,000

Scientists think there are at least 1 trillion species of tiny organisms on Earth. They think that almost all of these species have not been discovered yet.

Water is important for all living things, including tiny organisms that help us survive. In water, they clean and provide food for bigger animals. Inside us, they help digest food and keep us healthy by fighting off germs.

Biodiversity
AT HOME

No matter where you live, biodiversity is around you. Many backyards have various trees and plants. You can find birds, mammals, and insects in towns and cities. Natural areas like parks are full of wildlife. Even our pets are examples of biodiversity.

There are hundreds of dog **breeds** in the world. Dogs come in all shapes, sizes, and colors.

Many people keep birds as pets. In Australia, there are almost 4 million pet birds.

There are nearly 380,000 species of plants on Earth. Yards, parks, and roadsides are great places to see biodiversity.

The baobab tree grows in parts of Africa and Australia. It stores rainwater so it can survive the dry season.

Fascinating fact

Some people have pet spiders and insects. They keep ants in a habitat called a formicarium. It is like a big aquarium.

The prickly pear cactus has shallow roots that easily absorb rainwater. It stores water to survive long, dry periods.

The Norway spruce's thick bark protects it from cold temperatures. Its waxy needles retain water.

Backyards and GARDENS

In towns and cities, you can find biodiversity in many settings. It is in window boxes, greenhouses, and rooftop gardens. It is even in the traffic medians between streets and the shoulders of highways. All of these environments can have a variety of plants that provide food and shelter for wildlife.

Find out!

Can you find out the names of any plant species that grow in your area?

You can encourage biodiversity where you live by starting a compost pile. Composting food waste like fruit and vegetables is good for soil. Earthworms and other **decomposers** break down the waste. This returns nutrients to the soil.

Allotments provide a safe space for many creatures, including butterflies, bees, and birds. They help to pollinate plants and maintain a healthy ecosystem.

Gardens on balconies or porches can grow various vegetables, herbs, or flowers. They attract different insects and birds.

Gray squirrels have adapted to live alongside us in urban areas, but they still need access to trees to find food and build their nests, called dreys.

A window box or a hanging basket is a tiny ecosystem. It can be a home for plants and food for insects, such as **pollinators**.

There are more than 5,000 species of earthworms. Earthworms make soil drain better. They put nutrients back into the soil. This helps plants grow.

Cities Alive with
NATURE

Many people live in towns and cities around the world. It is important to help biodiversity grow in these urban environments however we can. Some methods include planting flowers in unused spaces and creating small outdoor parks for people to enjoy. City planners are creating green corridors. These are areas full of plants.

Singapore wants to make nature available to all. The city-state wants everyone to be no more than 10 minutes away from a green space.

Citizens are planting green spaces to aid biodiversity in Paris, France. These spaces will provide food and shelter for a variety of life.

Peregrine falcons have **adapted** to life in big cities. They nest on the ledges of tall buildings and eat various birds and rodents.

Almost one-third of Berlin is green space. Thousands of wild boars thrive in this huge city.

Fascinating fact

Rock doves are a common sight in urban environments around the world. These clever birds can recognize themselves in a mirror and sense human kindness.

More cities are making parklets. A parklet is a small seating area next to plants where locals can relax and cool off.

Helping
BIODIVERSITY

Biodiversity is important in places like farms and meadows. When farmers grow different crops, they attract insects like bees and ladybugs that keep plants healthy. Meadows containing flowers and grasses provide homes for butterflies, birds, and small animals. By planting different plants and leaving some areas to grow naturally, we can create spaces for wildlife to thrive.

Wild borders around fields act as natural highways for animals, providing food and shelter as they move between habitats.

Some farms grow crops in order to support the land. These farms protect the environment. They have high biodiversity.

Farms provide food and shelter for many wildlife species, such as this capybara in Argentina.

Pollinator meadows attract hummingbirds, butterflies, beetles, and bees. They provide food, shelter, and places to lay eggs.

Fascinating fact

Some coffee farmers are increasing biodiversity. They grow coffee in the shade of trees. The trees are the perfect habitat for many bird species.

WHAT CAN YOU DO?

1 Volunteer at a community garden where you live.

2 Make a bird feeder or a birdhouse to hang outside.

3 Shop at a farmers' market to support local farmers.

Swimming with
LIFE

Water is essential for all life, so it's no surprise that so much biodiversity is found in freshwater ecosystems. These habitats are home to at least 126,000 plant and animal species. Fresh water only covers around one percent of Earth's surface. Freshwater ecosystems include streams, rivers, lakes, ponds, swamps, and marshes.

Rice only grows in fresh water, in rice paddies. There are more than 40,000 different varieties. Rice feeds almost half the world's population.

Fascinating fact

Piranhas live throughout freshwater ecosystems in South America. Most species are **omnivores**. They eat insects, fish, worms, and seeds.

Electric eels are a type of fish. They can send an electric shock into the water. This can protect them from predators and help them catch **prey**.

Diving beetles store air in a bubble under their wing case. This lets them breathe underwater while catching tadpoles and small fish to eat.

Salamanders are found all over the world. Females lay their eggs in fresh water. Baby salamanders stay in the water until they are fully grown.

Close to one-half of all plants and animals live and breed in **wetlands**. But these ecosystems are disappearing. Farming and climate change are some of the threats they face.

Beside the SEA

Coastal ecosystems are found where the ocean meets land. **Estuaries**, wetlands, **tidal pools**, and beaches are all examples. Animals in these environments can live on the land, in the water, or both. Thousands of species live and thrive here. These ecosystems are high in biodiversity.

Ghost crabs dig burrows in the sand. This protects them from enemies and the **weather**.

Galápagos sea lions are social animals. They can often be seen relaxing on the beach. They mostly eat sardines, a type of fish.

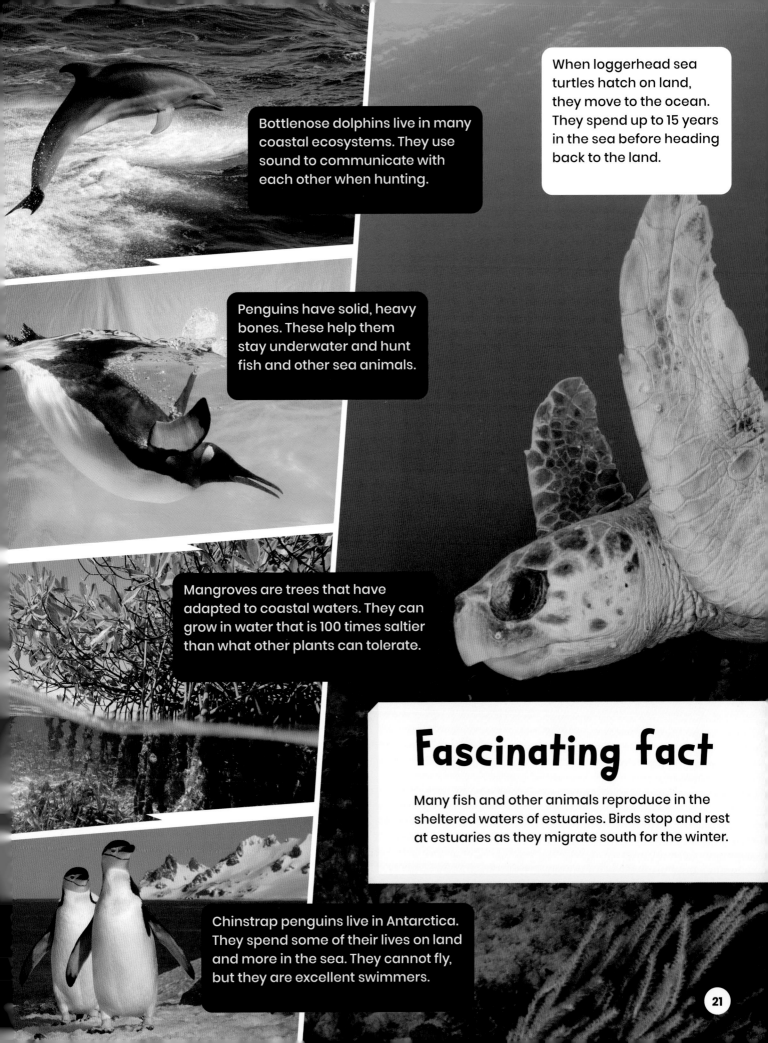

Bottlenose dolphins live in many coastal ecosystems. They use sound to communicate with each other when hunting.

When loggerhead sea turtles hatch on land, they move to the ocean. They spend up to 15 years in the sea before heading back to the land.

Penguins have solid, heavy bones. These help them stay underwater and hunt fish and other sea animals.

Mangroves are trees that have adapted to coastal waters. They can grow in water that is 100 times saltier than what other plants can tolerate.

Fascinating fact

Many fish and other animals reproduce in the sheltered waters of estuaries. Birds stop and rest at estuaries as they migrate south for the winter.

Chinstrap penguins live in Antarctica. They spend some of their lives on land and more in the sea. They cannot fly, but they are excellent swimmers.

Ocean
WONDERS

Almost three-quarters of Earth's surface is ocean. This huge ecosystem is full of biodiversity. Ocean ecosystems can range from coastal regions to deep sea trenches, and much more. We know of over 240,000 species that live in the ocean. Scientists think there are many more to discover.

Scientists have discovered that three deep-sea sharks use **bioluminescence**. The kitefin shark is the largest. It gives off a blue-green light, probably to camouflage itself.

Sponges are creatures that live in shallow or deep waters. Most are filter-feeders. They take in water and **filter** out animals and tiny organisms to eat.

There are over 17,000 species in New Zealand's waters. Over half of these species are only found in New Zealand.

New Zealand fur seals love to lie on rocky beaches and islands. They have thick, brown fur that helps to keep them warm in the water.

Hector's dolphins are the smallest and rarest dolphins on Earth. They are only found in shallow waters off the western coast of New Zealand.

Australia

More than 100 species of sea slugs live in the waters around New Zealand. Most eat seaweed.

Find out!

Can you find out the names of any marine animals that are native to your country?

New Zealand

From Floor to
CANOPY

Out of all the ecosystems in the world, rainforests have some of the most biodiversity. They are home to more than half of all Earth's animal and plant species. Life is everywhere, whether by a river, in the forest, or near wetlands. Let's explore the Congo Basin. This rainforest is found across six countries in Africa.

The **canopy** of the Congo Basin is made of the tall branches of mahogany, sapele, ebony, teak, wenge, and iroko trees.

Fascinating fact

Iroko trees can live for up to 500 years. Their wood is very durable and is often used for furniture and fencing.

Forest elephants are smaller and darker than savanna elephants. Their tusks are smaller and point down.

Bonobos are also called dwarf chimpanzees. They live south of the Congo River. They are an endangered species.

Tropical dogwood is a flowering plant that grows in West Africa, including in the Congo Basin. Its leaves stay green year-round.

More than 10,000 plant species live in the Congo Basin. The hot, wet, sunny environment is perfect for trees, vines, and other plants.

Crevices and CLIMBERS

Mountain ecosystems cover more than one-quarter of the land on Earth. They are on every continent. They are home to 85 percent of the world's amphibian, bird, and mammal species. They supply a lot of the fresh water that people need to survive. The Rocky Mountains are one mountain ecosystem. They pass through six western US states and into Canada.

Cliff swallows nest beneath horizontal rock ledges on the side of steep canyons in the foothills.

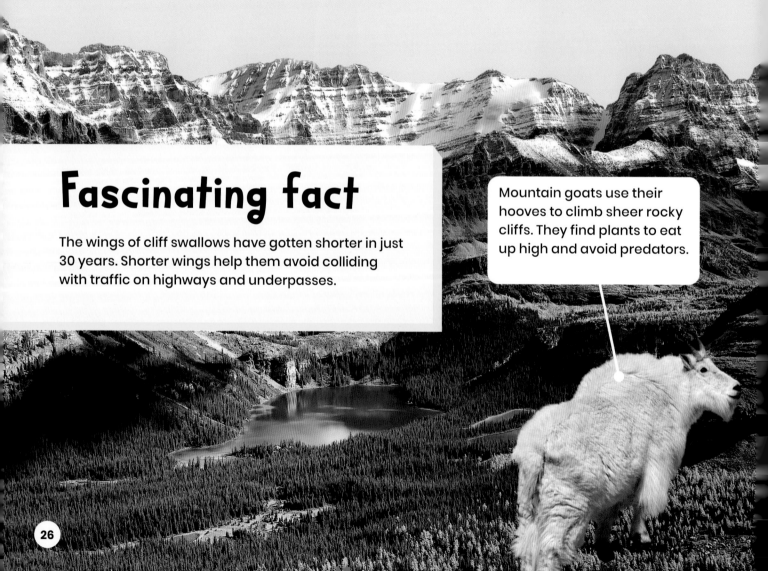

Fascinating fact

The wings of cliff swallows have gotten shorter in just 30 years. Shorter wings help them avoid colliding with traffic on highways and underpasses.

Mountain goats use their hooves to climb sheer rocky cliffs. They find plants to eat up high and avoid predators.

Indigenous Americans used the trunks of lodgepole pines to make tepees. The pines are long, straight, and lightweight.

In the mountain **tundra**, old man of the mountain flowers face east. This helps them survive the harsh westerly winds.

There are a variety of fir, spruce, aspen, pine, and juniper trees in the Rocky Mountains.

Lichen is a living thing that looks like moss. It grows well in environments where other plants can't, such as tundra.

Among the
GRASSLANDS

Grassland ecosystems cover up to 40 percent of the land on Earth. **Temperate** grasslands have warm summers and cold winters. Tropical grasslands are warm all the time. They mostly have dry and rainy seasons. All grasslands have a lot of biodiversity. The Pampas are vast grasslands in South America. They are in all of Uruguay and parts of Argentina and Brazil.

Long-tailed meadowlarks hide their nests in the tall grass to keep their eggs safe.

Geoffroy's cats have large ears to hear their prey. Their sharp claws grab lizards, rodents, and frogs from the river.

In the summer, strong winds fuel small wildfires. They burn everything in their path on the Pampas.

Cattails and reeds typically grow in wetlands. They have adapted over the years to the drier climate of the Pampas.

Pumas have strong legs and a flexible body. This helps them pounce on prey, from mice to guanacos.

Crops grow well in the rich soil and high **humidity** of the Pampas. But farming and **overgrazing** threaten this endangered ecosystem.

Fascinating fact

Guanacos are closely related to llamas. They rarely drink and take most of the water they need from the leaves of plants they eat.

Life in the
WILDERNESS

Deserts are ecosystems of extremes. Temperatures can reach over 100°F (38°C) in the daytime and then drop to below freezing at night. The soil is usually poor. There is little rainfall. But plants and animals have adapted to these conditions. Biodiversity is everywhere.

The Gila monster is a lizard that spends most of its life underground. This keeps it out of the hot summer heat.

Fascinating fact

The regal horned lizard squirts blood from its eyes. This helps protect it from predators.

The Mojave yucca is found across the Mojave Desert. Many desert mammals eat the yucca, including kangaroo rats and antelope squirrels.

Joshua trees have huge root systems. These help them grow in the desert. They can live for several hundred years.

Death Valley is in the Mojave Desert. It is one of the hottest places on Earth.

In the spring, you can see wildflowers across Death Valley. These plants wait for rainfall and cooler temperatures before blooming.

Polar SURVIVAL

Polar ecosystems are marked by harsh conditions. Ice, snow, cold temperatures, and high winds make them tough places for life to thrive. Incredibly, around 30,000 known species of plants, animals, **fungi**, and tiny organisms do just that. Even in these cold, desert-like environments, there is biodiversity.

Arctic willows grow in the Arctic. These plants provide food to caribou, musk oxen, and arctic hares.

Every year, arctic terns **migrate** almost 19,000 miles (30,000 km). They fly from the Arctic to Antarctica.

In the summer, arctic foxes have gray fur. It turns white in the winter. This camouflages the foxes and helps them hide from predators.

Cotton grass gets its name from its fluffy white flowers. It is food for migrating snow geese and caribou.

Antarctica has life along its shores and on some islands, such as penguins, petrels, and seals. On land, there are mountains, a cold desert, and ice.

Fascinating fact

Emperor penguins huddle together to beat the cold. They take turns so each one gets a chance to be in the warmest spot—the middle.

The tusk of a narwhal is actually a very long tooth. Narwhals use it to sense changes in water temperature and pressure.

Everyday
SCIENCE
Medicinal Plants

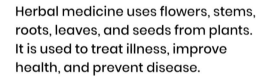

Ephedra is the oldest known medicinal plant. Its use dates back over 4,500 years. It was used to treat allergies, colds, and asthma.

For centuries, people have used plants to ease pain and fight disease. Hippocrates was a doctor in ancient Greece. He wrote about more than 300 species of herbs. He discussed how to use them to heal different **ailments**. Plants are essential in traditional Chinese medicine and Ayurvedic medicine, which began in India.

Herbal medicine uses flowers, stems, roots, leaves, and seeds from plants. It is used to treat illness, improve health, and prevent disease.

Today, almost half of all **prescription** medicines come from plants. For medicines that do not require a prescription, the number is around one-fifth.

Traditional Chinese medicine has been used for at least 2,000 years. Ginseng root is the plant that is used the most in treatments.

Ayurvedic medicine is an ancient practice. It dates back around 3,000 years. It often uses turmeric and aloe vera.

Indigenous Americans have used many plants as medicine. Many tribes used elderberry to treat fevers, colds, and headaches.

Everyday
SCIENCE
Medicinal Plants at Risk

Today, many medicinal plants are **cultivated**. These plants are specifically grown as medicine. **Botanists** estimate that up to 80,000 plant species are used for medicine globally. Ethnobotanists study plants around the world. They talk to local people to learn which plants have medicinal uses and understand their cultural importance.

The bark of the lapacho tree can help fight cancer. It grows in the Amazon.

Chamomile flowers are used to reduce swelling and pain. They are found around the world.

African wormwood is a common treatment for coughs, colds, flu, and malaria.

Around one-quarter of all medicines come from rainforest plants. **Deforestation** is destroying parts of the Amazon. Medicinal plants that grow here may go extinct.

Human development, pollution, and climate change can all harm biodiversity. Coastal areas, grasslands, forests, wetlands, and the plants within them are all at risk.

People around the world work to protect and restore ecosystems. It is a slow process. But every day, there are stories of new or rediscovered species.

What can you do?

Many healing plants grow in cities, parks, or backyards. Help protect native plants around you, such as nettles, echinacea, lavender, yarrow, and dandelions.

Let's EXPERIMENT!

BRING THE BUTTERFLIES

Seeing butterflies is a good sign that an ecosystem is healthy. Butterflies and moths make up around ten percent of all known species on Earth. This experiment will help to attract some to your outdoor space.

You will need:
- An overripe banana
- A butter knife
- Two pieces of card
- A pen
- Scissors
- Stickers
- Glue
- Craft sticks
- A tray

Be very careful when using scissors. You can ask an adult to help cut the shapes out for you.

1 Use a butter knife to carefully cut holes in the top and sides of the banana.

2 Draw two butterfly shapes on the card stock. Then cut them out.

3 Decorate your butterflies with stickers. Glue the craft sticks to the butterflies.

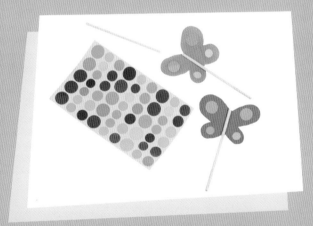

4 Place your banana on a tray. Stick your butterflies into the banana peel. Then, put the banana outside. Wait for hungry butterflies to come!

A MONARCH BUTTERFLY FEEDING ON A FLOWER

Did you know that butterflies have taste buds on their feet? They like to feed on nectar from flowers and sugary juices from fruits. Monarch butterflies live on different continents around the world. They eat lots of different nectar. They get moisture and nutrients from soil and gravel.

Let's EXPERIMENT!

MAGICAL MOLD

Mold is a type of fungus that grows in warm, damp places. It helps break down old food and dead plants. It is one part of a diverse and healthy ecosystem.

You will need:

- Two glass jars with lids
- Some pieces of fruit
- Access to a fridge

Be very careful with the moldy jars. Do not open them, and ask an adult to dispose of them safely.

1 Put half of the pieces of fruit in one jar and half in the other. Make sure the lids are tightly closed.

2 Place one of the jars in the fridge. Place the other somewhere warm, such as a windowsill. Leave the jars for one week.

3 After one week, look at the difference between the two jars. Which one is moldy? Leave the jars for a few more days.

4 After a few more days, observe the jars. Write down what you see. When you have finished, dispose of the jars safely. Do not take off the lids.

MOLD GROWING ON A MUSHROOM

Mold is one of nature's decomposers. Like earthworms and bacteria, it helps break down dead matter. This puts nutrients back into the soil. The nutrients help plants grow. Decomposers are the great recyclers of an ecosystem.

Vocabulary
BUILDER
Adaptations for Biodiversity

Read this report about adaptations in different animals. A behavioral adaptation is what an animal does in response to its environment. A physical adaptation can be a change in an animal's body. Or it can be something it does with its body to find food, find shelter, or escape an enemy.

"

Animals are equipped with special adaptations that help them survive in their environments. For example, giraffes have long necks to reach tall tree leaves, and arctic foxes have thick fur to stay warm in the cold.

Some animals also have unique ways to protect themselves. Pufferfish puff up to look big and scary, while skunks spray a stinky liquid to keep danger away. Kangaroos can jump really fast to escape predators.

Plus, some animals have special talents. Hummingbirds can hover in midair with superfast wing movements in order to drink flower nectar. Cheetahs can run incredibly fast to catch their food, and sloths move very slowly and hang upside down, making it hard for predators to spot them.

"

Behavioral	communication, forage, grouping, hibernate, manipulate, migrate, mimicry, symbiosis, tools, vocalization
Physical	antlers, arms, beaks, camouflage, claws, ears, feathers, gills, hair, markings on feathers or wings, mucus, **permeable skin**, pivoting eyes or heads, regeneration of tails, shapes of noses, slime, talons, teeth, thick fur, webbed feet

Nile crocodiles and Egyptian plovers have a **symbiotic** relationship. The plovers clean the crocodiles' teeth. This keeps their mouths healthy. The plovers get a good meal.

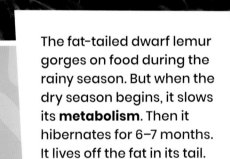

The fat-tailed dwarf lemur gorges on food during the rainy season. But when the dry season begins, it slows its **metabolism**. Then it hibernates for 6–7 months. It lives off the fat in its tail.

Choose a household pet, like a cat or a dog. Write a report about their behavioral and physical adaptations. How have they helped them survive in their environment?

Use the words in the vocabulary box above, the photos on this page and on page 10, and the example on page 42 to help you.

Glossary

Adapted Changed over time to better survive in an environment.

Ailment An injury or illness.

Algae An organism that can live in fresh or salt water and makes its own food.

Bacteria An organism that can't be seen without a microscope and lives throughout the environment.

Biodiversity The variety of living things in a habitat or ecosystem.

Bioluminescence The ability of a living thing to produce and give off light.

Botanist A scientist who studies plants.

Breed A group of plants or animals within the same species that look very similar.

Camouflage An animal's ability to blend in with its surroundings, used to hide from predators, or hunt prey.

Canopy The top layer of branches and leaves in a forest.

Citizen Someone who lives in a place, such as a country.

Climate The average weather conditions of a place over a long period of time.

Cultivated Grown, such as a crop.

Decomposer A living thing that breaks down dead plants or animals and recycles these nutrients back into the soil.

Deforestation The clearing of many trees from a forest.

Ecosystem A community of living things that interact with non-living things in their environment.

Endangered An animal that is at risk of going extinct.

Environment The place where a plant or animal lives and the interactions it has with the living and non-living things there.

Estuary A habitat where a freshwater stream or river meets the sea.

Filter To remove objects from liquid.

Fungus, fungi A simple organism that is not a plant or animal.

Habitat An environment where plants, animals, and other organisms live.

Humidity The amount of water in the air.

Metabolism The process in which an animal's body changes food into energy.

Microbiome The collection of tiny organisms that live on or inside a plant or animal.

Microscope A special tool that makes tiny objects easier to see.

Migrate To move from one area to another.

Mold A type of fungus.

Nutrient A substance that helps plants and animals survive and grow.

Omnivore An animal that eats plants and animals.

Organism A living thing.

Overgrazing The overeating by livestock of grass or plants in pastures, which prevents the plants from growing back easily.

Permeable skin Able for a gas or liquid to pass through.

Pollinator Something that helps move pollen between plants and fertilizes them, allowing them to reproduce.

Predator An animal that hunts and eats other animals.

Preening When birds clean and straighten their feathers using their beaks.

Prescription Used to describe medicine that you can only get with a doctor's permission.

Prey An animal that is hunted and eaten by other animals.

Species A group of living things that have similar features and can produce young.

Symbiotic When two different living things both benefit from their relationship.

Temperate Related to the temperate zone, marked by mild weather and a change in temperature from the summer to the winter.

Tidal pool A pool that forms along the coast when the tide goes out, leaving a pocket of seawater behind.

Tropical Related to the tropical zone, marked by high heat, humidity, and precipitation.

Tundra An area of land with no trees, not much vegetation, and a layer of soil that is always frozen—usually found in the Arctic regions or high on mountaintops.

Unique Used to describe something that is the only one of its type.

Urban An area where a lot of people live and work together, like a town.

Weather The temperature and other conditions, such as rain, wind, and pressure, of a place at a particular time.

Wetland Land that is covered by shallow water.

Index

Acknowledgments

The publisher would like to thank the following for their kind permission to reproduce their photographs:

(Key: a-above; b-below/bottom; c-center; f-far; l-left; r-right; t-top)

123RF.com: ljupco 41tr, mihtiander 11tl, tonobalaguer 5cb; **Adobe Stock:** Cavan 27tr, Roger de la Harpe 24, Maria T Hoffman 17tr, James 25crb, Matthew 17tl, Alexander Piragis 32-33tc; **Alamy Stock Photo:** adozenandonephotography 12crb, All Canada Photos / Wayne Lynch 4br, amomentintime 36clb, Yuri Arcurs 11br, Yuri Arcurs 34cr, art24pro 8crb, Iggino Van Bael 5tr, Antony Baxter 22clb, Scott Biales 16, Milous Chab 35br, Keren Su / China Span 18, Connect Images / Jouko van der Kruijssen 26tr, Roger de la Harpe / DanitaDelimont 25b, Xavier Dealbert 37cra, Design Pics Inc / Doug Lindstrand / Alaska Stock RF 7b, Gregor Fischer / dpa 15cra, Julian Eales 23tr, Chad Ehlers 32b, John Elk III 31tl, Martyn Evans 34clb, Emilio Ferrer 36cr, Marcel Gross 4-5, Frank Hecker 19cl, imageBROKER / Emanuele Biggi 4clb, imageBROKER.com GmbH & Co. KG / Alexander Schnurer 23tl, imageBROKER.com GmbH & Co. KG / Mara Brandl 30, imageBROKER.com GmbH & Co. KG / Marko von der Osten 43cr, Images & Stories 6b, J.D. 27tl, Juniors Bildarchiv / R304 43cl, Matthew J. Kirsch 11bl, Jason Knott 12bl, Marina_Lohrbach 34b, mauritius images GmbH / Bernd Römmelt 33tr, Megan McCarty 5cla, Mint Images Limited 21bl, Nature Picture Library / Kim Taylor 17cra, Michael Patrick O'Neill 21r, Christian Ostrosky 29tr, Edward Parker 24tr, Piemags / Nature 36br, Tom Reichner 26br, Gabriel Rojo 28, Rosa Russo 10tr, Scenics & Science 8b, Harold Stiver 14-15t, Scott Sady / tahoelight.com 31bl, Tetra Images / Inti St Clair 17br, volkerpreusser 16tr, Andre Seale / VWPics 23cr, Kelvin Aitken / VWPics 22tr, Michael Wheatley 19b, Roe Anne White 27crb, Alex Witt 14tr, Zoonar / Bernhard Kuh 10b, Claudio Santisteban / ZUMA Wire 29tl; **Dorling Kindersley:** Peter Anderson 37bc, David Fenwick 41br, Harry Taylor / Natural History Museum, London 5br; **Dreamstime.com:** Mihai Andritoiu 20, Yuri Arcurs 17bl, Yuri Arcurs 17bc, Borgogniels 9b, Paul Brady 27b, Patrice Correia 8-9tc, Nico Smit / Ecophoto 20tr, Efired 14clb, K Quinn Ferris 39br, Fotoeye75 36b, Andy Hoech 12-13bc, Ig0rzh 21tl, Tracy Immordino 12-13tc, Matthijs Kuijpers 7cra, Nelugo 26b, Nomadsoul1 36-37b, Jay Pierstorff 30cra, Positivetravelart 29b, Redfinch 13tr, Reimarg 19t, Gabriel Rojo 28cra, Seadam 21clb, SI Photography 7t, Thomas Stoiber 14bl, Jinaritt Thongruay 18tr, Sergey Uryadnikov 25tl, Sergey Uryadnikov 25tr, Viter8 19crb, Luka Vunduk 9tr, Wdnetagency 11tr, Wirestock 10bl; **Getty Images / iStock:** Alphotographic 32c, DragonImages 35tr, superjoseph 22b, Ron and Patty Thomas 31r; **Shutterstock.com:** Holly S Cannon 29c, Javier Cotin 33cra, Foto 4440 28bl, INTREEGUE Photography 14-15b, Jakub Maculewicz 20bl, MuhammadAsif6 32-33bc, Ondrej Prosicky 32bl

Cover images: *Front:* **Getty Images / iStock:** DigitalVision Vectors / Benjamin Toth t, E+ / gethinlane br; **Shutterstock.com:** Agus_Gatam cr, Joao Portal bl; *Back:* **Adobe Stock:** Cavan bl; **Alamy Stock Photo:** imageBROKER / Emanuele Biggi cl